NATURE'S CHILDREN

ANTEATERS

by Josh Gregory

Children's Press®

An Imprint of Scholastic Inc.
New York   Toronto   London   Auckland   Sydney
Mexico City   New Delhi   Hong Kong
Danbury, Connecticut

Content Consultant
Dr. Stephen S. Ditchkoff
Professor of Wildlife Sciences
Auburn University
Auburn, Alabama

Photographs ©: 123RF/Lajos Endrédi: 5 top, 27; Alamy Images/
Zizza Gordon: 11; Animals Animals/Alan G. Nelson: 18, 19; AP
Images/Mehgan Murphy, Smithsonian National Zoological Park:
28, 29; Dreamstime: 2 background, 3 background, 44 background,
45 background (Galina Dreyzina), 32 (Hotshotsworldwide),
2, 3 (Isselee); iStockphoto/jjgarcia03: 34, 35; Media Bakery/
Joel Sartore: 24, 25; National Geographic Creative/Kike Calvo:
5 bottom, 40; Science Source: 36 (Alan Root), 16, 17 (Francois
Gohier); Shutterstock, Inc./l i g h t p o e t: 8, 9; Superstock, Inc.:
cover (age fotostock), 6, 7 (Flirt), 1, 38, 39, 46 (Gerard Lacz
Images), 12, 13 (Juniors), 23 (Minden Pictures), 20 (Wayne Lynch/All
Canada Photos); The Image Works/The Natural History Museum: 31;
Thinkstock/Tom Brakefield: 4, 5 background, 14, 15.

Map by Bob Italiano

Library of Congress Cataloging-in-Publication Data
Gregory, Josh, author.
 Anteaters / by Josh Gregory.
   pages cm. — (Nature's children)
 Audience: Ages 9–12.
 Audience: Grades 4 to 6.
 Includes bibliographical references and index.
 ISBN 978-0-531-20667-6 (lib. bdg.) — ISBN 978-0-531-21660-6 (pbk.)
 1. Myrmecophagidae—Juvenile literature. [1. Anteaters.] I. Title. II.
Series: Nature's children (New York, N.Y.)
 QL737.E24G74 2014
 599.3'14—dc23   2014001508

All rights reserved. Published in 2015 by Children's Press, an imprint
of Scholastic Inc.

Printed in China 62
SCHOLASTIC, CHILDREN'S PRESS, and associated logos are
trademarks and/or registered trademarks of Scholastic Inc.

1 2 3 4 5 6 7 8 9 10 R 24 23 22 21 20 19 18 17 16 15

Anteaters

Class	Mammalia
Order	Pilosa
Families	Myrmecophagidae and Cyclopedidae
Genera	*Myrmecophaga, Tamandua,* and *Cyclopes*
Species	*Myrmecophaga tridactyla, Tamandua mexicana, Tamandua tetradactyla,* and *Cyclopes didactylus*
World distribution	Central and South America, as far north as southern Mexico and as far south as Paraguay and northern Argentina
Habitats	Forests, grasslands, and wetlands
Distinctive physical characteristics	Long, tubular muzzle with small mouth opening; extremely long, sticky tongue; no teeth; long, curved front claws; long tail; three species have prehensile tails
Habits	Uses long front claws to defend against predators while balancing on tail and hind legs; feeds by tearing open insect nests with claws and sticking its long snout inside; mainly solitary; except for mothers and their offspring, anteaters come together only for purposes of mating; mothers usually give birth to a single offspring each year, though twins are possible on rare occasions
Diet	Primarily ants and termites; also known to eat beetle larvae and bees; captive anteaters sometimes eat fruit

ANTEATERS

Contents

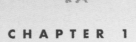

CHAPTER 1

Foraging in the Forest

Sunlight filters through the branches of the densely growing trees in the Pantanal wetlands of eastern Brazil. The wind blows softly as insects and birds fill the air with sound. Bushes and branches begin to rustle, and a strange, furry creature soon emerges in the clearing. At first, it appears as though the animal is walking tail first. However, its blinking eyes quickly reveal that its long, tube-shaped front end is actually its head! It is a giant anteater on the prowl for its favorite food: insects.

As the anteater ambles toward a rotting log lying in the tall grass, the long, thick fur of its tail drags along the ground. The anteater leans back onto its rear legs. It tears into the log with its long front claws. Termites come scurrying out of their damaged home as the anteater plunges its lengthy face into the hole and begins to feast.

A giant anteater can be identified easily by its long, narrow face.

An Unusual Appearance

Anteaters share many traits with other, more familiar mammals, such as cats and dogs. They have bodies that are covered in thick fur. They also have long tails and four strong legs, as many other mammals do. However, an anteater's unique head gives it an unmistakable appearance. Its long, tube-shaped face ends in a tiny mouth opening that is perfect for eating ants and other insects.

Anteaters vary greatly in size, depending on the species. The smallest anteaters weigh just 11 ounces (312 grams). They grow to a maximum length of around 17 inches (43 centimeters), including the tail. The largest anteaters are about the size of a large dog. They can reach lengths of up to 6 feet (1.8 meters) and weigh as much as 88 pounds (40 kilograms).

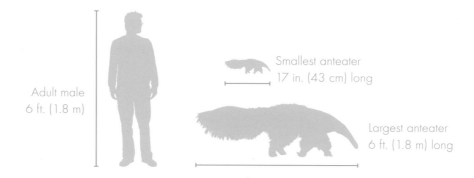

Adult male
6 ft. (1.8 m)

Smallest anteater
17 in. (43 cm) long

Largest anteater
6 ft. (1.8 m) long

An anteater's long snout allows it to reach into crevices to snatch insects.

Vermilingua Variants

Anteaters make up the suborder Vermilingua. There are four species within the suborder. The giant anteater is sometimes called the ant bear. It is the largest anteater species. Its fur is brownish gray, and it has a black-and-white stripe on its neck crossing from shoulder to shoulder.

The silky anteater is the smallest species. It is also known as the pygmy anteater or dwarf anteater. It has fuzzy, golden fur and a much shorter snout than other anteater species.

The remaining two anteater species are the northern tamandua and the southern tamandua. Tamanduas are also called lesser anteaters. They look a lot like giant anteaters. However, they are much smaller, and they do not have as much fur on their tails. Tamanduas have yellow, gray, or brown fur. Northern tamanduas have black, V-shaped patches of fur on their backs. Some southern tamanduas have similar markings, but most do not.

A silky anteater clings to a branch in a forest in Panama.

Anteater Abodes

Anteaters live throughout the forests, grasslands, and wetlands of Central and South America. Each of the four species is found within a different range and prefers different kinds of habitats. The giant anteater lives in the Amazon basin area of South America. It can be found as far south as Paraguay and Argentina. Instead of building a den, it finds a secluded spot to sleep and wraps the long fur of its tail around its body.

The northern tamandua ranges from southeastern Mexico into northwestern South America. Its southern cousin is found from the far north of South America to the northern portion of Argentina. Unlike giant anteaters, tamanduas sleep in dens. Tamandua dens are often in old logs or hollow trees.

Silky anteaters range all the way from southern Mexico to the countries of Bolivia and Brazil. They spend almost all of their time in the treetops. To sleep, they bed down in a nest of piled-up vines.

A tamandua nests in a hollow tree trunk with its cub.

CHAPTER 2

Built for Survival

Anteaters get their name from their habit of consuming massive amounts of ants, their favorite food along with termites. Because their prey are so tiny, anteaters need to eat a lot of them to get enough nutrients. A single giant anteater can gulp down up to 30,000 insects each day. Smaller species do not consume as many, but they still eat a lot of insects. Even the tiny pygmy anteater can eat 3,000 to 8,000 ants per day. Tamanduas devour as many as 9,000 per day. However, as many insects as anteaters eat, they never eat all of the insects living in a single nest or mound at once. They leave some behind so the insects can reproduce and continue to be a food source in the future.

Though ants and termites make up the bulk of an anteater's diet, anteaters also eat other foods on occasion. The soft larvae of beetles can make a tasty treat, and so can bees. Anteaters will sometimes even eat fruit that has fallen to the ground.

Giant anteaters eat at a single ant colony for about a minute or so before moving on.

The Nose Knows

An anteater relies on its senses to search out insects to eat. However, its vision is not very strong. Giant anteaters and tamanduas have very small eyes. A silky anteater's eyes are larger. This allows it to see in the dark, when it is most active. Anteaters' hearing helps them avoid predators, but it is not very good for finding insects.

Smell is an anteater's most important sense. It is around 40 times as strong as a human's! An anteater's nose looks a lot like a dog's nose. It is located at the end of the snout, just above the mouth. As the anteater walks, it keeps its snout pointed down toward the ground. This enables the anteater to pick up the scent of nearby insects and follow the trail to their nest or mound. An anteater's sense of smell also helps it detect poisonous types of ants or termites to avoid eating them.

A giant anteater tracks down an insect colony for dinner.

Worm Tongue

An anteater's body is perfectly suited to devouring as many insects as possible in a very short amount of time. All anteaters have long, curved claws on their front paws. When the anteaters locate an insect nest, they dig into it with these claws to create a bigger opening. Then they can stick their long snout inside.

Vermilingua, the name of the anteater suborder, comes from the Latin words for "worm tongue." This is because anteaters have long tongues that look like worms. The tongue is coated in sticky saliva. As the anteater flicks its tongue in and out of a nest or mound, insects stick to it and get pulled inside the anteater's mouth. Anteaters do not have teeth. They eat too fast to chew up their prey. Instead, their muscular stomachs grind up the insects after they are swallowed.

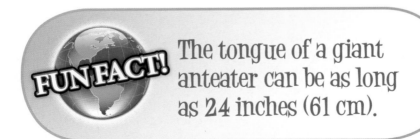

FUN FACT! The tongue of a giant anteater can be as long as 24 inches (61 cm).

Anteaters cannot yawn like people do. Instead, they yawn by sticking out their long tongues.

Crawling and Climbing

Anteaters walk on all fours. They are not very fast, though they can speed up to a jogging pace when necessary. Their back feet stay flat on the ground as they walk. They walk on the outside of their front feet, with their claws curled up. This keeps their claws from scraping against the ground, which would wear them down. It also keeps the claws from poking into the anteater's palms.

Giant anteaters spend all of their time on the ground. Tamanduas and silky anteaters are good climbers, though. Their tails, which do not have hair on the tip, are prehensile. This means they can grip branches and act as an extra limb as the anteaters climb. Silky anteaters spend almost all of their time in trees, while tamanduas spend around half of their time on the ground.

FUN FACT! Anteaters are able to swim. Their long faces work like snorkels!

A tamandua uses its prehensile tail to grip a branch
for balance as it moves through a tree.

Fighting with Feet

Anteaters do not face many threats as they calmly wander through their home ranges in search of food. However, predators such as pumas and jaguars sometimes hunt them. Smaller anteaters, such as tamanduas, must also watch out for eagles and snakes.

Because anteaters are not fast runners, they must hold their ground and defend themselves when a predator attacks. Normally docile, a cornered anteater quickly turns into a fierce fighter. The anteater rears up onto its back legs, using its tail to stay balanced. It shows off its dangerous claws and makes roaring and hissing sounds at its enemy. It slashes its claws through the air in an attempt to scare the predator away. However, if the predator decides to attack anyway, the anteater is more than capable of battling its foe. Giant anteaters have even been known to kill jaguars when forced into a fight!

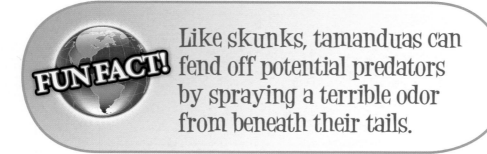

FUN FACT! Like skunks, tamanduas can fend off potential predators by spraying a terrible odor from beneath their tails.

A tamandua's sharp claws and strong front legs make it a dangerous foe.

CHAPTER 3

An Anteater's Life

Anteaters are not very social creatures. They prefer to spend most of their time alone. Anteaters are usually sleeping or wandering their home range in search of food. The size of an anteater's home range varies greatly depending on the species. A giant anteater might roam across 6,000 acres (2,428 hectares) of land, while the silky anteater generally stays within about 12 to 25 acres (5 to 10 ha). The tamandua wanders around 185 acres (75 ha) on average. Anteaters' home ranges often overlap with each other. Anteaters are not territorial, and they do not fight if they enter each other's home ranges.

Because anteaters are mostly solitary, they do not need to make noise very often. Most communication takes place between mothers and their pups. Anteaters can make a variety of hissing, snorting, or sniffing sounds with their trunks. They are also capable of roaring when trying to scare off an enemy. Silky anteaters can make high-pitched whistling sounds.

A giant anteater curls up to sleep, its tail draped over its body like a blanket.

Mating Season

Generally, anteaters are only seen together when a mother is caring for her babies or when it is time to mate. When a female anteater is ready to mate, she begins releasing special scents. Male anteaters use their powerful noses to follow these scents to the female. After mating, both giant anteaters and tamanduas part ways. Male silky anteaters, however, remain to help their mates care for pups.

After about six months, the mother is ready to give birth. Anteaters usually have just one pup at a time. However, twins are also possible in rare circumstances. Baby anteaters have full coats of fur. They look much like adult anteaters, only smaller. Almost as soon as it is born, a baby anteater climbs up onto its mother's back. Because its fur is the same color as its mother's, the baby stays hidden as it rides around. This keeps it safe from potential predators.

FUN FACT! Anteaters sleep up to 15 hours a day.

A giant anteater cub yawns as it clings to its mother's back.

Providing for Pups

At first, baby anteaters only climb down from their mother's backs to **nurse**. As they grow older, they spend less time there. They also rely less on their mother's milk for food. They learn how to crack open insect nests and gather food by watching their mother. By the time they are around 6 to 12 months old, baby anteaters no longer rely on their mothers for transportation. However, they still stick by their mother's side. A young anteater might stay with its mother for up to two years. Pups sometimes strike out on their own at an earlier age if their mother becomes pregnant with a new pup.

Young anteaters are old enough to have pups of their own when they are between one and four years old, depending on the species. Most anteaters live around 10 to 15 years in the wild. Giant anteaters typically live longer than their smaller cousins. Silky anteaters live only around three years.

Young anteaters learn important survival skills
in the years they spend with their mothers.

CHAPTER 4

Ancient Animals

Anteaters are part of a larger group of animals known as xenarthrans. Xenarthrans include all of the animals in the orders Cingulata and Pilosa. Cingulata consists of armadillos. Pilosa is made up of anteaters and sloths.

Xenarthrans are grouped based on the construction of their lower backbones. These backbones have extra joints that make the animals' hips and lower back stronger. Xenarthrans rely on the strength of their back legs while using their front legs to dig or climb.

The earliest known xenarthran species first appeared between 65.6 million and 55.8 million years ago. They once occupied a much wider range than they do today. Some species reached as far north as what is now Alaska. Many ancient xenarthrans are now extinct. Scientists have learned about them by studying fossils. Other xenarthrans have changed considerably over time. Today, in addition to the four anteater species, there are 17 kinds of armadillos and six types of sloths.

The giant ground sloth, which lived between 1.8 million and 10,000 years ago, was an early anteater relative.

Slow and Steady

Though they might not look much alike, sloths are anteaters' closest relatives. Sloths are found throughout the forests of Central and South America. They have four long limbs that end in long, hook-shaped claws. While their arms and legs make sloths very good at climbing, they make it extremely difficult for sloths to travel on the ground. The only way sloths can move on land is to drag themselves along the ground. As a result, they prefer to spend almost all of their time in trees. They come down from their treetop homes around once each week to urinate and defecate.

Like anteaters, sloths are slow moving and solitary. They spend most of their time resting and searching for food. Sloths are herbivores. They eat leaves, shoots, and fruit as they climb through the treetops. Because all of these foods are filled with water, sloths do not need to spend much time drinking.

FUN FACT! Some ancient sloths were as large as today's elephants!

A young three-toed sloth rests in a tree in Costa Rica.

Armored Cousins

Armadillos are another anteater relative. They have a slightly wider range than sloths or anteaters, with one species reaching as far north as the southern United States. The word *armadillo* is Spanish for "little armored one." They got this name because these fascinating animals are covered in a series of tough, protective plates known as a carapace.

Armadillos vary widely in size. The largest species, the giant armadillo, can grow up to 5 feet (1.5 m) long. The smallest armadillos, such as the pink fairy armadillo, are only around 6 inches (15 cm) long. Like sloths and anteaters, armadillos have long, sharp claws. They use these claws to dig burrows in the ground, where they rest during the day. At night and in the very early morning, they come out and search for food. An armadillo's diet consists mainly of insects and their larva, along with some plants.

Armadillos are the only mammals around today that are covered in protective plates.

CHAPTER 5

Allying with Anteaters

Like all life-forms, anteaters play an important role in keeping their ecosystem healthy. Because of their diets, they are especially important for keeping insect populations in check. Without anteaters around to eat tens of thousands of ants and termites every day, these insects would quickly become too numerous. This would throw off the balance of the ecosystem, causing problems for other plants and animals in the area.

Unfortunately, anteaters face many potential threats to their survival. Most of these threats come from humans. For example, anteaters are commonly hunted by the people of Central and South America. Some of these hunters kill anteaters to use the animals' fur and meat. Others target anteaters for sport, or capture and sell them as pets.

Silky anteaters and their relatives are an important part of a healthy ecosystem.

Disappearing Dwellings

The biggest problem that anteaters face is habitat destruction. Human populations have been growing larger year after year for a very long time. As human populations grow, people need more space to live. They often deal with this by taking over wild areas that were once home to many plants and animals. Humans clear entire forests away to make space for houses, farms, and businesses. They also cut down trees for lumber and for making paper supplies such as napkins, cardboard packaging, and paper towels. As this happens, wild creatures such as anteaters are forced into smaller and smaller spaces, and their food sources are reduced.

In recent years, this rapid human expansion has brought another threat to anteaters. As people settle in areas that were once wild, they also build roads so they can drive from place to place. Many of these roads travel through areas where anteaters live. As the anteaters try to get from one part of their home range to another, vehicles often hit them.

Today, some anteaters risk crossing roads and highways to reach food.

Aiding Anteaters

None of the four anteater species are in immediate danger of being wiped out. Of the species, giant anteaters are the most at risk of seeing their population begin to dwindle. Some experts believe that the species' numbers could decrease by as much as 20 percent over the next 10 years. Most conservation groups believe that anteater hunting should be limited to avoid too many animals being killed.

Even though anteaters are not endangered, we must be careful to make sure that the situation does not get worse. Anteaters need plenty of space to survive in the wild. We can help them by avoiding behavior that is bad for the environment. Recycling and using fewer paper products are two good ways to prevent habitat destruction. Like all living things, anteaters deserve our respect and attention. With a little help, they will continue to thrive long into the future.

A scientist holds a recently rescued giant anteater cub.

Words to Know

carapace (KAYR-uh-pays) — a hard case or shield covering the back or part of the back of an animal

conservation (kahn-sur-VAY-shuhn) — the protection of valuable things, especially forests, wildlife, natural resources, or artistic or historic objects

den (DEN) — the home of a wild animal

docile (DAH-suhl) — calm

ecosystem (EE-koh-sis-tuhm) — all the living things in a place and their relation to the environment

endangered (en-DAYN-jurd) — at risk of becoming extinct, usually because of human activity

extinct (ik-STINGKT) — no longer found alive

fossils (FAH-suhlz) — bones, shells, or other traces of an animal or plant from thousands or millions of years ago, preserved as rock

habitats (HAB-uh-tats) — the places where an animal or plant is usually found

home ranges (HOME RAYN-jiz) — areas of land in which animals spend most of their time

larvae (LAHR-vee) — insects at the stage of development between eggs and pupas, when they looks like worms

mammals (MAM-uhlz) — warm-blooded animals that have hair or fur and usually give birth to live young; female mammals produce milk to feed their young

mate (MATE) — to join together to produce babies

nurse (NURS) — to drink milk produced by the mother

orders (OR-durz) — groups of related plants or animals that are bigger than a family but smaller than a class

predators (PRED-uh-turz) — animals that live by hunting other animals for food

prehensile (pree-HEN-sile) — adapted for seizing or grasping, especially by wrapping around

prey (PRAY) — animals that are hunted by another animal for food

pups (PUPS) — the young of certain animals

saliva (suh-LYE-vuh) — the watery fluid in an animal's mouth

solitary (SAH-li-ter-ee) — not requiring or without the companionship of others

species (SPEE-sheez) — one of the groups into which animals and plants of the same genus are divided; members of the same species can mate and have offspring

suborder (SUB-or-dur) — a group of related plants or animals that is bigger than a family and smaller than an order

territorial (ter-uh-TOR-ee-uhl) — defensive of a certain area

Habitat Map

PACIFIC

OCEAN

NORTH

AMERICA

ATLANTIC

SOUTH
AMERICA

Anteater Range

ARCTIC OCEAN

EUROPE

ASIA

AFRICA

PACIFIC OCEAN

OCEAN

INDIAN OCEAN

AUSTRALIA

Find Out More

Books

Antill, Sara. *Giant Anteater*. New York: Windmill Books, 2011.

Borgert-Spaniol, Megan. *Anteaters*. Minneapolis: Bellwether Media, 2012.

Visit this Scholastic Web site for more information on anteaters:
www.factsfornow.scholastic.com
Enter the keyword **Anteaters**

Index

Page numbers in *italics* indicate a photograph or map.

(Index continued)

About the Author

Josh Gregory writes and edits books for kids. He lives in Chicago, Illinois.